CLARE BRENNAN

HOW HAPPINESS HAPPENS

The Ultimate Guide on True Happiness, Learn
Everything You Need to Know on How You Can Be
Truly Happy in Life

Descrierea CIP a Bibliotecii Naționale a României
CLARE BRENNAN
   HOW HAPPINESS HAPPENS. The Ultimate Guide on True Happiness, Learn Everything You Need to Know on How You Can Be Truly Happy in Life / Clare Brennan. – Bucharest: Editura My Ebook, 2020
   ISBN

CLARE BRENNAN

HOW HAPPINESS HAPPENS

The Ultimate Guide on True Happiness, Learn Everything You Need to Know on How You Can Be Truly Happy in Life

My Ebook Publishing House
Bucharest, 2020

TABLE OF CONTENTS

FOREWORD

"Happiness is when what you think, what you say, and what you do are in harmony." - Mahatma Gandhi

Everyone wants to learn the secrets on how to be truly happy in life. For sure, right now, most people in this world are still in pursuit of happiness, a journey that many of them have probably started right from that very moment when they learned about the concept of "happiness."

Did you ever wonder what it really takes to be truly happy? Many people tried pursuing relationships, money, and success, and most of them have reached that point when they have realized that happiness does not really come from the outside, or from the world where you live in. In all essence, happiness is something that comes from deep within you, lying in that secret place within yourself, waiting for you to finally tap it and release it from its prison.

Happiness is something that has long been present inside you. Finding happiness inside yourself is like peeling off the layers of onion, with each layer representing your thoughts, fears, and negative beliefs. As you slowly peel away each layer (who you are not), you will gradually reach its very core (who you are). And right there and then, you will find your purpose and meaning in life. You will finally discover yourself and learn the real meaning of happiness.

For you to be truly happy, you need not lock yourself up inside a closet and meditate for the rest of your life. To be truly happy, there are some things that you have to learn first and in this Empowered Happiness Bible, you are bound to unravel what it takes to finally know the meaning of HAPPINESS. Get all the info you need here.

Empowered Happiness Bible
Everything You Need To Know To "Truly" Be Happy

CHAPTER 1

INTRO

Synopsis

Happiness is a state of one's mind. You do not look for it. You do not even have to chase it. Happiness, in truth, lies within yourself, starting from you and ending at you. In the simplest essence, happiness is about getting back your true nature. While other people try to look for happiness through their wealth, career, money and success, you have to understand that happiness is something that you choose for yourself.

So, what are the basics of happiness? What are the things that you can do in order for you to truly start being happy with your life?

The Basics

Be in Control and Take Possession

Your body is composed of hundred trillion of cells, all of which are answerable to you and you alone. You are basically these cells' commander in chief and they are working constantly not for the benefit of other people, but only for your own benefit. For these cells, you are the only person that exists. To start on your journey to happiness, you first need to be in control of these cells, take possession and be responsible for these cells for in so doing; you also become the master of both your mind and body.

Be Yourself

Newborn babies practically share the same level of happiness the moment they have been given birth to this world. However, their happiness level starts to change once they get older. One basic rule in order to become happy is for you to remember that your fundamental nature is soft, vibrant and full of enthusiasm, energy, and love. You must never compare yourself with other people because you are exceptional and unique. And this uniqueness is something that you need to explore. If there is one thing about you that you do not like, never put the blame on your parents, on other people and most importantly, on yourself. What you need to do is acknowledge its existence and accept it as it is. Instead of lamenting, what you should do is exert some efforts in order for you to eliminate this one thing that you do not like and by this, you can expect to be happy.

Empty Yourself

If you are truly determined to be happy, you also need to free your mind and body from all negativities. Remember that there is nothing negative on earth, only your thinking makes things that way. Get rid of fear, frustration, ego, tension, hatred, anger and stress from your system. Be aware of your destination and imagine yourself getting there. Relax. If things are bound to come, they will come, only if you want them to.

After you have learned how to be in control of yourself, how to be yourself and how to empty yourself, the next step is for you to fill yourself with as much positive energy as you can. Fill yourself with hope, kindness, compassion, positive feelings, gratitude, desires and love. As you do so, you can finally tell yourself that happiness is just within your reach.

CHAPTER 2

WHY PEOPLE ARE SO SAD TODAY

Synopsis

"Every man has his secret sorrows which the world knows not; and often times we call a man cold when he is only sad." - Henry Wadsworth Longfellow

With everything happening around the world, with all the wars, natural calamities and other kinds of catastrophes that befall on the people, it is no longer a surprise that many of them end up sad, or worse, even depressed.

If you feel down or you got the blues, then, you should know that you are not alone. Every single person in this world gets sad. When you are sad, you will surely feel that that sadness is bound to last forever. But more often than not, sad feelings do not really last that long – several hours, or even a day or two probably.

Sadness

Sadness – What is It?

When you feel sad, the whole world might seem unfriendly and dark to you all of a sudden. Deep inside you, you feel that hurt that seems to crush both your spirit and your heart. Most of the time, you find yourself crying, with the tears difficult to stop. For most people, crying alone can already make them feel better. The moment sadness starts fading away, that is the time when you feel as if the heavy and thick blanket has finally be lifted off your heart, and you feel happiness all over again.

The Natural Reasons for Sadness

It is only natural for a person to feel sad every now and then. Maybe you were not able to get that one thing that you have always wanted. Maybe you suddenly missed the presence of a person close to you. You were probably rejected by someone or maybe, you simply do not feel that good about yourself.

People actually have a lot of reasons why they feel so sad at one point in their lives. One of the most common reasons for sadness is loss. Losing someone you love or something important to you will surely induce feelings of sadness. Whether it is the loss of a loved one or a pet or moving to a brand new city and leaving your old friends behind, this kind of losses are enough reasons for a person to be sad.

While relationships are the best source of fun and happiness most of the time, these can still make a person sad. A lot of kids today end up fighting with other members of their family, particularly their parents, as they struggle growing up and gaining independence. Relationships in the workplace can also bring about sadness in most people today, especially when you are constantly having discussions with your colleagues or your boss does not seem to notice your hard work.

But probably the most usual reason why a lot of modern men and women today feel sad is because of self-image, or the way that you feel about yourself. Adults in particular are not totally happy on how they look. They feel inferior with others whether in school, at work and other aspects of their lives. It can be easily observed especially when talking with the opposite sex, with some people feeling shy to do so because for them, they are not that good enough.

While it might be pretty much understandable why many people today feel sad, there is actually no reason for them to dwell on this feeling. At the end of the day, being happy is something that they should strive to achieve, for many reasons.

CHAPTER 3

WHAT IS TRUE HAPPINESS?

Synopsis

"True happiness is to enjoy the present, without anxious dependence upon the future, not to amuse ourselves with either hopes or fears but to rest satisfied with what we have, which is sufficient, for he that is so wants nothing. The greatest blessings of mankind are within us and within our reach. A wise man is content with his lot, whatever it may be, without wishing for what he has not." - Lucius Annaeus Seneca

Are you happy? If you are, how happy are you?

True happiness refers to the measurement of two kinds of happiness, namely experienced happiness and remembered happiness.

True Happiness

Experienced happiness pertains to those moments of relief, bliss, laughter, or joy that you have experienced within a day. Imagine your friend asking you randomly during lunch time about what you are doing and how happy you actually are at that very moment. That is experienced happiness, the kind of happiness that comes from the things that you do for a particular period of time.

On the other hand, remembered happiness refers to how you think about yourself in general. This is how you will answer that million dollar question "Are you happy with your life?"

This is how you remember those years you had in high school, the vacations that you went to, the holidays you have spent with your whole family, the early days of childhood with other kids, your history of jobs, or even your divorce. Remembered happiness is pretty much like the bigger picture or perspective on your state of happiness.

It is not surprising that experienced happiness and remembered happiness do not match all the time. For instance, millionaires in general have higher rate for their remembered selves compared to those people who only earn $50,000 each year.

However, a millionaire might have more responsibilities in life. He may experience more pressure in his work, with a larger house to run and a spouse who is more demanding.

It only goes to say that even if they are earning millions, these people might have lesser moments of spontaneous happiness during their day to day lives, and living their lives less happily. Meanwhile, an ordinary employee who considers himself as less happy since he lacks the kind of luxury that he has been dreaming of might, in reality, experience great bliss and pleasure with their jobs, with their family or with their hobbies, thus, they tend to have more blissful moments in their day.

Experienced and remembered happiness might be entirely different things but once you have happy moments in your past and your present, then, you can say that you have reached the so-called true happiness.

CHAPTER 4

WHAT IS THE EMPOWERED HAPPINESS MINDSET?

Synopsis

Do you want your life to be happier? Do you want your relationships with other people better than before? Do you want your business to be successful? Well, the real secret to all of these lies on your mindset. Weird as it may sound, you are living in a world in which things happen depending on what you think.

This is something that most people fail to realize. Whether you actually believe this or not, this is something that works similarly for everyone. By focusing on the things that you do not want or complaining about those negative things in your life, more negativity tend to enter your life. But if you start to focus more on things that you want and think about all the positives happening to your life, you also bring in more of that.

What Is It

Happiness, as they always say, is a choice, which means that if you choose to be happy, then, you will be. Happiness is a kind of choice that you make and create for yourself. It is not something that depends on creating the happiness of other people or getting their approval. In reality, the level of your life's happiness has nothing to do with the things that other people say or do, even if you feel like it actually. Happiness is not something that you capture through the affirmation or actions of others.

Can you really make up your mind to be happy?

The answer is YES. The empowered happiness mindset is set on the principle that despite the things that happen to you or whatever dire circumstances you might be in today, you can still be happy.

Your happiness comes from within and happiness can only be experienced if you have established a connection to your core self, that part of you that lies deep within and never changes even after all those year.

If you decide that you will be happy right from your core, then, you are the one who have the power to identify the degree of happiness that you will experience.

If your core self is not being overpowered by hormonal or chemical challenges or overshadowed by your mind's incessant chatter, then, there is a high chance for you to experience the so-called "unconditional happiness." Your core self has the ability to stick to its decision of being happy and not falling apart or giving in to discouragements once it encounters less than perfect conditions.

When you learn living from your core, it is not impossible for you to be happy even during the toughest of times because you already know how you should hold on to those good times and chase all the bad away. With an empowered happiness mindset, you will know how you should let life to happen and stay open to wallowing in bliss of happiness whatever your circumstances might be.

CHAPTER 5

TRADITIONAL HAPPINESS
IDEAS VS. NEW AGE IDEAS

Synopsis

When you dream of happiness, you probably dream of that one place where suffering is absent – a place with no guilt, anxiety, melancholy, and mood swings. With the present way of life of many people, most of them surely look forward to that one day when all their mental battles and worries will subside – that one golden day when purely positive things will take place and there will be no more reasons to experience pain, tension, and sorrow.

Ways To Look At It

But unfortunately, all these things are just part of a mythical place. This is a kind of place that society would like you to believe exists, just another gold pot sitting at the end of that proverbial rainbow, which, when found, will give you security and wealth.

The traditional happiness ideas revolve around this mythical place with perceived security and comfortable luxury. However, there is no way for this ideal to come to reality all because of one law of life, which can be easily summed up in a single word – change.

Change is everything that life knows. Your assets, your moods, your relationships, your liabilities as well as the other conditions of your existence are not going to stay constant, whatever your cultural idea might make you believe.

Disaster, death, unforeseen misfortune, conflict, disease, heartbreak as well as the simple anxieties of your everyday life will continue and disrupt what you perceive to be peace of happiness.

The new age ideas about happiness dwell on the principle that even though the traditional happiness ideas might be mythical and somewhat boring, still, there is a chance for you to find a deeper and truer state of being. As a human being, your greatest satisfaction will lie not in the constancy, but in the transformation.

For the modern era, true happiness is about accepting, embracing and even laughing at your pain. Its aim is to understand that your pain is a natural result of the changes in your life and it is a crucial precursor to your growth.

CHAPTER 6

WHAT DOES EMPOWERMENT FOR HAPPINESS MEAN TO YOU (HOW TO SET GOALS)

Synopsis

Right from that very moment of your birth, you never got the chance to choose the kind of life that you will live. Back then, it does not even matter a bit. Being a newborn, you had no care at all about those things that matter to the grownups around you. But when you reached that point when you already understand the difference between white and black, happy and sad, good and bad, when you find yourself trying to feel good, it is when you finally start to wonder. What is the real definition of happiness? How you do find it?

What Does It Mean

Dear friends, happiness is not something that you can just purchase from a nearby store because if it can be, then, all people in this world will surely get their pockets empty and their banks broken on buying happiness each time they feel the need for it, both for themselves and those close to their hearts. It only means that people with no money will also be deprived of the chance of being happy.

But of course, this is not the case. Happiness is something springing from within, a product of all your actions. And despite being intangible, happiness is not necessarily elusive.

So, before you wallow yourself in negativity and completely giving up on your search for happiness, you need to feel empowered and for this, you have to know how you should set goals so that you can be happy, truly happy.

First, you have to determine the things that make you feel bad. Identify each one of them by writing them down on a paper. If you want to be genuinely happy, you have to identify the reasons for your sadness because it is the only way for you to face the issues head on.

While laughter is considered as the best medicine, it will surely not feel right, especially when all you want to do is cry your eyes out or scream at the top of your lungs.

Happiness will only come if you will address those things that induce negative feelings such as sadness, guilt, anger, and so on and so forth.

After writing down the things that make you feel bad, the next thing to do is right down those that make you feel good, small or big alike.

Of course, you cannot do all things that you want for there will always be things that will hold you back from doing so but there is no need for you to fret.

You will only have to manage your time and set your priorities. In goal setting, you will learn managing your time so that you can fulfill all your duties and at the same time, do those things that can make you happy.

And last but not the least, you should never let other people wipe away that hope that you have in finding real happiness. When they tell you that it is impossible for you to find it, prove to them that they are wrong.

Empowerment for happiness is about not letting others bring you down and fighting for your right to be happy. After all, you are entitled to it and all you need to do is choose.

CHAPTER 7

WHY ADOPT THE EMPOWERMENT MINDSET FOR HAPPINESS

Synopsis

Having a happy mindset is very powerful and is not something that you should underestimate. In just a single day, you have thousands of different thoughts, and only some of these are actually happy and positive. It is not a secret a happy person has happier and more positive thoughts compared to an unhappy person. When you think positively, you are also given with an improved clarity as well as courage and confidence in facing the day that lies ahead.

Why Do It

Adopting the empowerment mindset for happiness helps you in determining your own path instead of following others. Sad to say that through the negative thoughts like jealousy, fear and anger, people are thrown off their path, losing their ability of thinking and acting effectively.

But if you try to have a happy mindset as opposed to an unhappy one, you can certainly attain greater things in your life. You will have the chance of being a happier person overall.

When you are happy, a more exciting future waits ahead of you while being unhappy and thinking negative thoughts places you stuck in a vicious circle where you continue to be afraid and fearful, causing you to act defensively. It is something that tends to push other people away from you, creating more problems as you become lonelier and more afraid than ever.

Following the empowerment mindset for happiness as you travel in the path of life can help make you feel better, which will then lead you to become a stronger and even more stable person. With this kind of mindset, you will be completely in control and not someone who will be easily pushed around by others.

While there will always be bad days and negative things that will happen, learning to see the positive side of these things and learning how to avoid yourself from being dragged by such situations will help you stay on happiness' path.

Thinking is an automatic thing, which means that changing your thoughts can take effort and time, though it is not necessarily impossible. By adopting the empowerment mindset for happiness, you will learn how to automatically think in a positive way, which will then lead to a 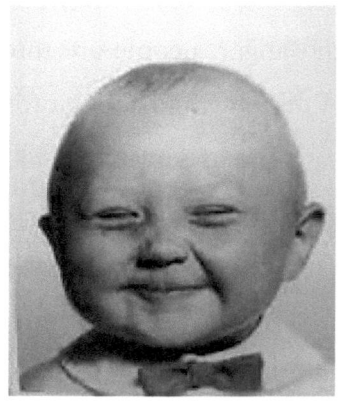 longer, healthier and happier life full of happy thoughts only.

CHAPTER 8

TIPS FOR BECOMING EMPOWERED
FOR HAPPINESS

Synopsis

"Happiness is not a possession to be prized, it is a quality of thought, a state of mind." — Daphne du Maurier, Rebecca

In their search for happiness, a lot of people search for it not within themselves but in other people. Many of them assume that things such as a good job, more money, better relationships and others will give them the happiness that they are searching for.

But, the truth is, you can only find true happiness and contentment if you will look within yourself and you will learn how to be your self's best friend. It means that you need to care, trust, and love yourself the way you care, trust and love those people near your heart.

Here are several tips that are guaranteed to make you empowered for happiness that you might want to keep in mind:

Tips

- Give positive rewards to yourself. If you have done something that you are proud of, try giving yourself even with just a small reward. If possible, never wait for praises from others because if it does not come, you will end up feeling resentful. Patting your own back every once in a while won't hurt and in fact, this is a great feeling which will surely stay with you within a long period of time.

- Instead of pulling yourself down, try lifting yourself up. If there is one thing about yourself that you do not like, do something to alter it. If it cannot be changed, then, accept it as it is. Never go for negative self-talk because you lessen your chances of changing for the better if you are already filled with negative thoughts.

- Learn forgiving yourself. Surely, you will not scold a child over and over again for a mistake that he did so never do such a thing to yourself as well for it will not do you any good. Forgiveness is a gift that you can endow yourself if you made a mistake. After that, try figuring out the lesson that you learned, using it as an inspiration in making better choices in the future.

- Take pleasure in your successes. Many people can still clearly remember the details of embarrassing, painful or depressive events that took place several years ago. What if you try doing exactly the same thing with the wins and successes that you had in the past? Instead of wallowing on your downfalls, why not remember your accomplishments and trials and keep their memory with you? Thinking about these successes at least once every week will surely make you feel good.

Never forget celebrating all the wonderful qualities that you have! The best and most important tip for becoming empowered for happiness is learning to love yourself for as you do so, you will also be able to love others around you and they will also start to love you even more!

CHAPTER 9

THE GOOD AND BAD ABOUT THE EMPOWERMENT MINDSET FOR HAPPINESS

Synopsis

No matter where you live, or whatever race you might belong to, it is easy for one to get stuck in a rut, emotionally and intellectually, which can cause unhappiness. A lot of studies have revealed the causes as well as effects of happiness, with numerous benefits being associated to being happiness, professionally as well as personally.

Your happiness can be negatively affected by outside forces, some of which are out of your control, such as bothersome coworkers, loss of a loved one, or even the weather.

But, there will also be those forces which are controllable and during such cases, happiness becomes a choice. It is easy and common to be wallow and be engulfed in self-pity once the blues start to call, but adopting the empowerment mindset for happiness will be very beneficial for you.

The Good And Bad

One good thing about this mindset for happiness is that you will actually be more motivated to face every single day. You will not experience that laziness of waking up every morning and instead, you will be more energized to face the day. You will feel happier and if you are happy, you will also be more optimistic, allowing you to focus only on those good things with your life.

This empowerment will also help you to become more creative and productive. An unhappy person is more distracted, less productive and more sluggish.

They also have higher chances of getting sick. But if you are happy, you will feel better, be more energized and have an improved focus that will increase your creativity and productivity. If this happens, you can easily and successfully finish all the things that you are set out to do while still having some spare time to do the things that you really enjoy.

If you are a happy person, more people will start to like you. It is good to be work and be around a happy person who smiles more often and has a more uplifting and positive attitude that inspires others.

Unhappy people can bring negativity to those around them, causing unhappiness and negative thoughts, something that is unpleasant for those around them. On the other hand, happiness is contagious, making other people around you much happier, which will then make you more positive and uplifted.

The empowerment mindset for happiness only has good things about it and there is nothing bad about it for after all, there is surely nothing wrong with being happy, is there? This kind of mindset is something that needs to be adopted for everyone because if it happens, then, the whole world will surely become a much happier and better place to live in.

CHAPTER 10

CONCLUSION

"Happiness depends more on the inward disposition of mind than on outward circumstances." — Benjamin Franklin

At the end of the day, there is only one thing that this Empowered Happiness Bible wants to teach you, and that is, the source for happiness is just lying within you. Real and genuine happiness can only be yours, whatever the circumstance you might be in right now, by looking inside you.

While short term happiness can be yours with the pleasant circumstances, this can actually chronically distract you in your pursuit for the long term type of happiness.

The primary ingredients for you to obtain real happiness are summarized as follows:

- Recognize that your emotions and thoughts are not "you" in essence for these are just products of the mind which can come and go as they please.

- Never categorically abandon short-time pleasures but be more selective in opting for long term happiness over the short term pleasures every time you feel the need to choose.

- Consider your heart as the instrument that will guide you in making the right choices which will help you in finding happiness for long term.

- Try to give your mind with undistracted rest and time. Set aside some time in your calendar for peace of mind that can be used for contemplation and creating new spaces within your mind.

While living in this world is far from being perfect and there will always be times when you will feel the weight on your shoulders, it must not stop you from being happy. As being said over and over again throughout this book, happiness is actually a choice, not something that just "happens." You, and not other people, will decide when you will be happy. Being happy is a matter of will. If you willed yourself to be happy, then, there is no reason for you not to find that happiness.

May this Empowered Happiness Bible serve as your guide and inspiration in reaching and experiencing genuine happiness! Never look for happiness anywhere else. Instead, look inside yourself and in there, surely, you will find that one thing that you have long been searching for!

Printed by Libri Plureos GmbH in Hamburg, Germany